THE AMERICAN POETRY REVIEW/
HONICKMAN FIRST BOOK PRIZE

The Honickman Foundation is dedicated to the support of projects that promote spiritual growth and creativity, education and social change. At the heart of the mission of the Honickman Foundation is the belief that creativity enriches contemporary society because the arts are powerful tools for enlightenment, equity and empowerment, and must be encouraged to effect social change as well as personal growth. A current focus is on the particular power of photography and poetry to reflect and interpret reality, and, hence, to illuminate all that is true.

The annual American Poetry Review/Honickman First Book Prize offers publication of a book of poems, a $3,000 award, and distribution by Copper Canyon Press through Consortium. Each year a distinguished poet is chosen to judge the prize and write an introduction to the winning book. The purpose of the prize is to encourage excellence in poetry, and to provide a wide readership for a deserving first book of poems. *The Search Engine* is the fifth book in the series.

The Search Engine

The Search Engine

Kathleen Ossip

WINNER OF THE APR/HONICKMAN FIRST BOOK PRIZE

THE AMERICAN POETRY REVIEW/PHILADELPHIA

Distribution by Copper Canyon Press/Consortium.

Library of Congress Catalogue Card Number: 2002106630

ISBN 0-9718981-0-3 (cloth, alk. paper)
ISBN 0-9718981-1-1 (pbk., alk. paper)

First edition
Designed by Adrianne Onderdonk Dudden
Composed by Duke & Company

Acknowledgments

Many thanks to the editors of the following journals, which first published these poems:
American Letters & Commentary: "Ballade Confessionnelle," "The Search Engine"
The American Poetry Review: "My Dark Night," "He," "A Conception" / *The Antioch Review:* "Nursling" / *Barrow Street:* "The Nature of Things" / *Bathos Journal:* "The Genius" *Can We Have Our Ball Back?:* "Nobody talks about the moon anymore," "Little America," "Riddle" / *The Cream City Review:* "My 20th Century" / *Crowd:* "The Simp," "The Essentialist" / *Denver Quarterly:* "My Luvox," "Landscape" / *Elixir:* "Three Prayers" *Fence:* "Air" / *The Journal:* "My Analysis," "My Best Self" / *The Kenyon Review:* "The Flat Tire," "The Pleasure of Your Company" / *No Roses Review:* "Rhyme" *The Paris Review:* "The Fatso," "The Rosebud," "The Witness," "The Seer," "The Enthusiast," "The Consultant" (*under the title* "Eight Rants"); "Babyland" *St. Luke's Review:* "In the Atrium" / *Slant:* "57th Street" / *Slope:* "The Pouter," "Aquí se puede comprar camisetas perro" / *Verse:* "Once"

"The Nature of Things" *appeared in* The Best American Poetry 2001, *Robert Hass and David Lehman, eds. (Scribner).*

My deepest gratitude to Susan Wheeler, David Lehman, David Trinidad, Robert Polito, David Baker, and Richard Howard: magisterial guides. And to Derek Walcott: for opening the door. And to Mark Bibbins, Nancy Nalven, Rebecca Reilly, Soraya Shalforoosh, Patrick Pardo, Mia Berkman, Stuart Feinhor, Katheryn McDonald, and Matthew Pritchard: for "precious communications at crucial moments." And to my family.

« For Robert »

CONTENTS

INTRODUCTION

It is a difficult mandate, almost an obscene one, to choose one
victor from a swarming mob of nine-hundred submissions, win-
nowed finally down to twenty, to find that victor unquestionably
the best, unless the throb of genius in a particular manuscript,
or rather typescript, is such that it leaps with a sudden, silvery
flash from a widely netted catch. Then everything surrounding
it pales as the rainbow horde loses the colors of its scales. This
metaphor will only go so far. Sufficient to say that the patient
fisherman or angler with the dangling, bobbing lure of a prize
hopes that the hooked trophy will redeem his patience, even
his exasperation at the dull sheen and repetition that he cruelly,
never angrily, rejects. Thus, *The Search Engine* leapt from the
pile with wriggling force, it tautened the line, and its own lines
caught the light of genuine intelligence.

    It is a book, enough of fishes now, that admits its influences
easily, using pop songs and academic quotes in a self-confessed,
even parodic rummaging in old or corny texts for its own voice.
It is unembarrassed about models, which in the old craft was
called homage, like this catalogue, an accelerated version of
Frank O'Hara's "The Day Lady Died":

> when across the aisle someone comments There's more than ten
> keys on the keyboard, I'm sorry and a smell of sterno
> comes from the buffet the busboys are setting up
> beyond which glass capsule elevators drop
> weightlessly and through the skylights with
> their tracery of old rains show curdled clouds
> and a skyscraper perpendicular
> and the lozenges of fluorescent lights therein
> and maybe the office workers will see the torchères

gentle, elegiac, the one finger on the keyboard picking out the
theme with its muted conjunctions is not as easy as it sounds.

O'Hara is less adjectival, but what I like is the conspicuous effort to broaden its range beyond the individual, self-consoling pathos. There are poems with a fastidious hilarity:

> We're having drinks in the
> Sputnik Lounge, in daydresses and
> ballerina slippers. (She's dating a
> pilot.) Hey, Ma, I say,
> y'know Rock Hudson, that
> actor you like? Well I just
> read in *Tittle-Tattle*...She
> hits a high note like
> a wigged castrato.

Everything, hitherto beautifully balanced by the pseudo-tension of the prepositional line-endings, parodic of its own meter, via W. C. Williams, suddenly collapses from the stress and ends in an a-metrical screech, including the macho image of the dissolving screen star and his fan who has suddenly reversed herself into a powdered eunuch.

Granted that all this may come out of a given diction, that of the University journal, even of the creative writing class, with that as a base, the rhythms are rapidly accommodated into the varieties of one voice, that is, into what Eliot pretended to deplore because of his own evasions, a personality, one that is marinated in the fashionable as well as its opposite, the satirical. The jocularity hides serious pain.

> If we could only stay in life's frank, deft moments,
> I thought on the occasion of my nth breakdown.

The poetry of nerves, of which the best exponents are Berryman, Plath, and even to some degree but more mutedly because of her exterior cool, Elizabeth Bishop, is self-evidently, truly

American, and this poet is a fine recorder of its devastating little complexities, as in a brilliant sequence called "Fourteen Rants":

The Wet Blanket

You've one douce backstory, a dowdy
yearning for Archimedes' lever.
You're once, twice, three times a toastmaster.
The family lived—didn't they?—in
a house crowded to bursting with books,
pictures, and music. Case, rested. Bones,
broken. Frankness, appreciated.

and

The Simp

Cuando en el train, en el ghost train,
con los guns y los handbags, you drip
ice sweats. Cuando en la booth, you talk
long time. Some dumb hoodoo man dagnabbed
you for your sins! You ain't no psychic.
You ain't no shopper. Cuando en la
deli, you get a ham omelet.

The eye is restless and relentless, a detail-devourer, a silent machine that has developed, like a diary, a hunger for subtleties. Perception of this kind, after a while, becomes almost an affliction, an interior tape in the brain that revolves, even in sleep with its merciless record. In "The Magic Husband" there is an acknowledgment to Berryman's similar fever of helpless industry.

(1)

Oh, we cavort. *A little less poise, please.*
The shower-crud, the plangent peonies!

He chisels at the oaken escritoire
his paperwork—his toy, his dream, his art—

and hums as if to all America
a dope impromptu on the sound of schwa.

The last line is incomprehensible to me, but with the poem's careful descent into banality, even idiocy, the point—the futility of art—edges into a pompous nonsense, a sarcastic mockery of itself. The "schwa" itself, whose meaning we don't care about, is via Wallace Stevens's cartoon-like phonetics, but this is a dangerous poem, not merely a comic, absurdist one. It conceals the poet's own impending collapse into incoherence like a character in Beckett.

The tragic, obliquely, looking sideways into a mirror, then turning away alarmed, is what *The Search Engine* discovers in the diurnal. That diurnality, its hedgings and its customs, sound as if it is the pattern of a not-so-good housekeeper, without the morbidity of her models, Plath and Sexton, but with the humor of redemptive vigor, even coarseness. The best thing about the author is that she would make good company, always at her own expense. We can admire good and great poets without wanting to have breakfast with them. At her acutest she is irresistible, and some of the work can be cute in a superficial, dismissive tone, but continually, you feel like quoting her, because her indebtedness is so natural, so fresh and so open. Via e. e. cummings:

He spoke, and drank rapidly a glass of water.

Via Berryman:

His thought made pockets and the plane buck't.

Her own:

You opened her blouse, and the gates rang.

Finally:

The Enthusiast

Why, it skitters like a water bug!
That is, the hassock you call a brain:
spongy pink hillocks draped in black lace.
Where are the snows that melted under
your poignant feet, galoshed? Whatever
became of your sparkling bitterness?
What happened to the housewife-poet?

Even if it is an androgynous, dragged-out question, the answer is
that the poet has done extremely well, thank you.

Derek Walcott
January 2002

The Search Engine

In the Atrium

Ha! I'm a vessel of pure experience in
the marmoreal yet midwestern hauteur of the lobby bar
of the opulence-is-democracy-in-action Times Square hotel
where the deaf-mute salmon-colored plastic clock
signs teatime with lacy black hands and roman numerals
Barcelonesque and revolves in a postmodern cutout
belltower consisting of four effete girders and
a black steel A-frame pinnacle and groups of women
in full makeup drink vodka and fruit juice and play
shopping striptease, peeling back tissue to uncover
the latest sweaters and cityscapes, and kids from O-
klahoma, with the kinetics of boredom, dash
across the veiny floor, Air Jordans squeaking,
and another group of women, bussed downstate
for a bargain matinee, want never to rise
from hunter green leatherette club chairs and I note
that I was brought up to dress like them—plaid shirts,
stickpins, ski jackets, oxfords—but that was before
I became a vessel of pure experience
and I note the fringed jazz-age torchères and the flower
arrangements afflicted with gigantism and verisimilitude,
Nile green and fuchsia silk dendrobiums
wilting even before their uppermost petals
relax into fullness, and one of the upstate women—
the youngest one, with the cockscomb bangs and the niecelike
impassive aspect—undramatically lets a mouthful
of tea dribble back into the white stoneware mug
and the maître d' shuffles over and switches on
the electronic player piano which begins to ring
"Matchmaker, Matchmaker" and the man and woman behind me
drawl and balk in a lazy dialogue
about the meeting they've just left and territory
review and we should meet Ted tomorrow, 'kay?
and now "'Tis May" on the piano so I pretend

to stretch so I can get a glimpse of them—
two padded torsos leaning and rolling in tandem
like a ball and socket joint, his porcine but nicely
groomed in black suit, gray cubist tie dotted with peppercorns—
and he tells her There's this little goom-bah Italian
place a couple blocks down, they stand up to go
to dinner to the tune of "If I Loved You"
with an obbligato bass reminding us of
the one-way flood of time and as he walks by,
his hand on the small of her back, he isn't so porcine
though certainly paunchy but a face toothsome as an olive,
eyes Slavonic which sting my heart and he
strokes my hair and kisses me but that's
impossible (I'm a vessel etc.)
when across the aisle someone comments There's more than ten
keys on the keyboard, I'm sorry and a smell of sterno
comes from the buffet the busboys are setting up
beyond which glass capsule elevators drop
weightlessly and through the skylights with
their tracery of old rains show curdled clouds
and a skyscraper perpendicular
and the lozenges of fluorescent lights therein
and maybe the office workers will see the torchères

1

I always tried to stick as much as possible to what really happened.
—Elizabeth Bishop

My 20th Century

We are having tea and
dobosh torte, my mother
and I, dressed in hobble
skirts and buttoned boots,
in Peacock Alley of the
old Waldorf. (She thrives on
luxury.) Hey, Ma, I say,
this Sigmund Freud says neuroses
arise from repressed sexual
fantasies! She clatters her cup
in a kind of a trance.

We're having tea and Ritz
crackers, my mother and I,
dressed in chemises, shingled and
bobbed, in the sitting room
of my first apartment. (She's
a little jealous.) Hey,
Ma, I say, Susan Anthony
won! We're getting the vote!
She moves like a brown
bird on a brown branch.

We're having tea—the sugar
is rationed—my mother and
I, wearing trousers and snoods,
in a soldier's canteen. (I'm
her supervisor.) Hey, Ma, I
say, have you seen that
movie about Scarlett O'Hara, the
heroine who proves, once and
for all, that a woman
can be hard as nails

yet loved by millions? She
hefts a widget, not too friendly.

We're having drinks in the
Sputnik Lounge, in daydresses and
ballerina slippers. (She's dating a
pilot.) Hey, Ma, I say,
y'know Rock Hudson, that
actor you like? Well, I just
read in *Tittle-Tattle*...She
hits a high note like
a wigged castrato.

We're taking spoonfuls of blue-
green algae in the solarium
of the nursing home (I'm
getting tired; her joints are
sprightly). We're dressed in
leopardskin aerobicwear. Hey,
Ma, I say, there's this
guy who says all religions
derive from a shared mythology.
What do you think? She
swivels and rides
away on her trike.

I'm eating bread and water
alone, naked as the day
I was born. Hey, Ma,
I say, though she's not
around, you won't believe this.
Physicists say that in
addition to a yes and a

no, the universe contains a maybe.
Off in the distance, under the stars,
she moves like a platypus,
neither here nor there.

1970

Zish-zish
goes the gibbous
insect. They bring the lawn
in rolls. Now is what I have, or
will get.

Ballade Confessionnelle

(Plath and Sexton)

They're out of the dark's ragbag, these two—
two cramped girls breathing carelessly.
No day is safe from news of you,
though the oarlocks stick and are rusty,
heavy and rigid in a pool of glue.
The night nurse is passing.
The world is full of enemies.
I couldn't stop looking.

They tell you to go, and you do
with the help of the red-haired secretary.
You say your husband is just no good to you.
That's what it means to be crazy.
The permanent guests have done nothing new.
I confess I am only broken by the sources of things:
a pane of dragonfly wing, when they left me.
I couldn't stop looking.

The skulls, the unbuckled bones facing the view!
In a dream, you are never eighty.
They're the real thing, all right: the Good, the True
that glide ahead of the very thirsty
and the locked drops rising in a dew.
The cup of coffee is growing and growing.
So much for psychology.
I couldn't stop looking.

Fading out like an old movie,
it was not a heart, beating.
I love them like history.
I couldn't stop looking.

Rose of Sharon

Her banal, her tomfool, her carnivalesque and don't you forget it.
Her Extreme Violet in a fever-hut. Sentient plastic cum phallic pistil.
She's like, *What've you got to do with living and dying?* Now, she began
in New England when March blew in. Began with unmitigated
drives. Began with the pleasures of adulthood. Pity was the rain that
fell and swelled, a pity next-door to passion. The Lord lifted up his
hand and gave her a forlorn hope, and did she ever pop amid the
squiggly, figgy leaves. As for me, I was bored, I was bored with the
Lord. I thought *she* could be all to me. She of the astral kisser. Then
Star-face got all victimy, then Star-face says *Accept. Float. Let time
pass.* Then I sniffed her in the downtown playground. I looked over,
under, and in that shrub but couldn't find Truth nowhere. This gaud
needs love of. Love of the least. Love of the least sentimental kind.

My Analysis

In ballet, there are only primary relationships.
I lay down prepared to acknowledge that,
hugging my ribcage with a ballet-like gesture.
That's all. You supply the story.

After a while I felt much worse. The maples
went from yellow to blue and back.
Maybe I had no inmost soul,
only a crimped, crabbed, bitter kernel.

Talk was out so it must have been
coming back, and the shrink all but said
By this sign shalt thou conquer. There now,
that's not exactly Iphigenia in Aulis. Pretty soon

I got up and joined the gang on the lawn
playing statues as in the Golden Age.

My Aesthetics

1965, and all gathered in London to say:
We like what our skill can do to you.
When I write my hypertext I'll remember.
Anglophilia goes beyond content.

(The joy of the love object, said the DES daughter.
The joy of small things.
In the present decade, in the feminist collective
her exclamation points took the edge off.)

It was a faux nostalgia, the pathos tapered
everlastingly in the parlor of blond wood.
The shaping imagination will find something to shape.
I sat and read. I tried to sit and read.

For that poetry I had to wear two pairs of glasses.
Hail, William Empson. Hail, treasury of verse.

My Luvox

The lilt of suffering sensibility's everywhere.
Chlorophyll's warm on sebaceous skin.
You can find it in the catalogue of spa gifts.
But to literalize helps no one.

A lumber dies. Jonquils file on the floor.
If I were your mother, I'd take you on walks
and teach you *Ulmus, Quercus, Acer saccharinum,*
the drooping catkins of the genus *Betula.*

Once I promised I wouldn't be irritable.
I stood on the helipad, my coattails lolloping,
as a chopper came down. I watched.
That was surely my Big Mistake.

I'd been in trouble with the city already,
and the grand deficit waved wily and wry.

My Dark Night

The girl in the red jumpsuit and her flabby ass moved off.
She went medieval, she went Imagist, she was on a roll.
To inscribe between the lines, to fill the gap!
Instead I spent my time staring at the bastards.

The recognition that is gradual, but the shock sudden,
is a form of consumer anxiety—
Are We Classic or Romantical This Year?
And the mutt on the pavement, a transfiguration—

The raw happened, the raw always happened.
I spelled vigor with a u and gray with an e.
Toiling at the anvil of Strike-Not-the-Wrong-Note,
I studied lyrics for profundity:

Walking down the street that June I was robed Jesu.
The halibut on my plate, Lao-Tzu.

My Ativan

But it's too far from singing! I said.
A guy named Jim was walking anesthesia,
nab and huff two unexpected verbs.
When I left the party, everybody was praising everybody else.

Come go with me on my Viennese quest—
The words turned to slang even as Jim spoke.
For the life of me I couldn't make myself interesting;
a Heineken and a Gothic cross levitated down.

In the moment before the door closed I got my things
(whimsy masking fear, impudence mixed with rare
good humor) and slugged a pot of silk impatiens.
The Heinie beat the cross onto the floor.

Someday, it's true, our citizens shall have a glittering beauty.
I want my destiny whole, and now.

My Best Self

It's the one in Malibu, or the one
with bitten nails, or the one that asks,
Which struggled harder, my infant or the surf?
Such reluctance seems, in the end, self-protective.

I believed that I wanted a paean, of all things.
I guess I had a really expansive mind.
When she put her fingers in my mouth I breathed,
Sweeter than hope of heaven, hellion—

that being something I hadn't read.
Sheer plainness. We blew bubbles
at each other, and scenery became circumstance.
I swear I always wanted so much more.

If we could only stay in life's frank, deft moments,
I thought on the occasion of my nth breakdown.

The Complaints of Maria Goretti

1890–1902. After her father died, she took over the care of five younger siblings while her mother farmed their land in the Pontine Marshes south of Rome. On July 6, 1902, Alessandro Serenelli, a boarder, tried to rape Maria and, when she resisted, stabbed her to death. In 1950, Pius XII canonized her as a martyr.

A scrap of paper found in her apron

Maria Goretti. Donna Maria.
Signorina, Signora.
The oak trees heave themselves from sand.
Napoli, Corsica, Roma.

Friday, see if you can get
fish trimmings. Pick zucchini.
Don't walk near the port at night.
Don't forget linguine.

Potty-train Vincenza soon.
A red silk skirt, a mirror.
Delphiniums are heaven-blue.
Dump slops, beat rugs, cook supper.

The Tyrrhenian Sea lies off the west
coast of Italy.
Best friends: Paola, Angela.
Scrub floor. Maria Goretti.

On her last words

A synapse spread—a child's beach hole
whose sands collapse at once to fill
it up. The words fell in like that:
It is a sin. God does not want it.

To Alessandro Serenelli, on appearing in his prison cell

You're forgiven, friend. And look: I've shed my worldview.
No longer do I tremble when you wag your...dagger.
Accept these daisies. Know they just don't grow in anger.

That evening in the kitchen when you stuttered "Fuck me"—
O sweet space pierced by stars (but you can't see them, can you?)
in no fanatic pattern neither cursed nor lucky.

On her canonization

In a room as big as ten houses, cherubim on the ceiling,
a choir choired in Latin. The little pope blessed me:
"Not for the Christian faith, but for the Christian life."
Eighty-eight-year-old Mama, Carlo, Vincenza on wobbly jeweled
    chairs.
Alessandro, scared (forgive me) stiff. They say he repented
after my visit and lived, among monks, the Christian life.

To those who call her "Saint"

I hear your sighs and moans:
Hear my antiphon.
Let's say you have a dream.
Your panic grows extreme.
You attempt a scream
but it's sibilant as steam.
Meanwhile, monsters teem.
Can mere intent redeem?
A resolute black ant
totes a bit of twig or plant

until he tries and can't.
An obstacle, adamant,
adjusts the path aslant.
Direction's variant.

On her representation in art

White robe. White rose.
Pink face. Creamed hands.
Sad stare. Wet lips.
Red lips. Kohled eyes.

Cut throat. Breast buds.
Gold hair. Not me.

On miracles attributed to her

Barely cold, they begged me warm my fingers
curing lung-sick women, maimed war veterans.

Azure was my mark, a bluish aura
would surround the injured limb or organ.

Virtuosity as well as virtue
I exude: I leave them wanting more than

anyone can give—not I, not Jesus.
Love, sincerity; they flow unbidden.

On the afterlife

Sometimes I think that I've
become a word.
A sign whose sound protects
its mystery.
Could heaven be the rasp
of skin on skin?
Matter mattered. Meaning
meant. But here?

On her last day

Alessandro swaggered in
pelvis first, reeking of salt.
I was boiling the pasta,
cleaning my face in the steam.
Half-breath. Nothing's decision.
The neighbors always said how
good I was. Meant: how silent.

2 Fourteen Rants

So many surround you, ringing your fate,
Caught in an anger exact as a machine!
                              —Delmore Schwartz

The Fatso

Venus is rising. She's muttering,
A sober chick is a sullen trick.
When it comes to bliss, I dream it;
you live it. Indolence, you've left
pee stains all over the almanac.
Minipads all over the palmtop.
Beercans all over the landscaping.

The Seer

4 I C U R M T. Color
of maize your bathrobe, you vowed the time
was at hand, daughter of the lower-
middle class, celestial recycler!
O U R Z 1 4 me, you vowed,
saline, between the hours of twelve and
three, when Jesus bled upon the tree.

The Wet Blanket

You've one douce backstory, a dowdy
yearning for Archimedes' lever.
You're once, twice, three times a toastmaster.
The family lived—didn't they?—in
a house crowded to bursting with books,
pictures, and music. Case, rested. Bones,
broken. Frankness, appreciated.

The Pixie

Your osmosed piquancy is its own
reward. Walking sine wave, your selfhood's
pointy. Clatter to the left of you,
feng magazines to the right of you,
your beverage tastes mighty fragile.
Which water would an aesthetician
approve? Zygotic fog. There, you're drenched.

The Rosebud

Hello, artifice central? Nah, I
didn't hate it when you (infanta)
and Mr. X frugged in the dooryard
so uncultivated and *real slow*.
You dig everything magenta,
flying mammals, and the number ten.
Hello, diadem? Pick your poison.

The Demi-Vierge

Old Half-moon fixed the bong like a pro.
With abandon, you gave yourself to
a burger deluxe. Where the charcoal
gray night winnowed the elms, where the wind
pricked at your belief system—this kiss, this
kiss, O.K., but a *bambino*? I.
e., To use it up, or use it wrong?

The Genius

Such Christian copacetic babblings!
What comes after postmodern if not
your peculiar brand of Greek-key rave?
Your spaniel Duchamp, now a phantom,
romps in fields of quinoa, so you write.
Such Buddhist pheromones. And this from
a goddamn genius. How reticent!

The Pouter

Inspiration for a clapping game
or finger exercise: tot up the
nimrods clogging the escalator.
At the psychological moment
you'd ream out parasols, or Peru.
In the end it was just a *perfect*
thing to do, that hail of hot metal.

The Simp

Cuando en el train, en el ghost train,
con los guns y los handbags, you drip
ice sweats. Cuando en la booth, you talk
long time. Some dumb hoodoo man dagnabbed
you for your sins! You ain't no psychic.
You ain't no shopper. Cuando en la
deli, you get a ham omelet.

The Stay-at-Home

Passion's not enough; you've also learned
to be a little canny. Dinner,
a symphony in dried herbs. Goodly
tunes. Dirndl of matchless suede. A weep
supreme. In a German-speaking place,
things might very well be different.
You opened her blouse, and the gates rang.

The Witness

Rather than gather your smattering
of apostles, you stayed bravely put.
Rather than dither, you studied the Sino-
Italo-Russian pact. A treatise
ensued. It was wack. Time out of mind,
you studied Nipponese tortureware.
An odor ensued. It wasn't kind.

The Enthusiast

Why, it skitters like a water bug!
That is, the hassock you call a brain:
spongy pink hillocks draped in black lace.
Where are the snows that melted under
your poignant feet, galoshed? Whatever
became of your sparkling bitterness?
What happened to the housewife-poet?

The Consultant

The story: A guy with soulful brown
peepers hires a pert gal who wavers.
Result: One spirit, restless in life
as in death, sings for a moment, then
lies broken in two. Cause: You with your
snazzy advice, your French sinecure,
you fixing things as God fixes them.

The Essentialist

"This, this is what the dying are like!"
As I listened in the park I knew
there's nothing square about your sleek slide.
In the middle of the lake: "The soul
is violent. If it leaks at all,
it leaks in screams." Quel grand slam, quel null
set. It was to be a pleasure jaunt.

3

*I myself...would rather be told
too little than too much.*
        —Marianne Moore

Air

If I can't have you
   (and could if only too)

hunger will the when.
   Treasure still till then

the tender net of strange,
   and rend lamenting change.

The river in the boat
   most simple, most remote

rushed before we knew.
   If I can't have you

closes now the where,
   captivates the dare,

cages tarried why.
   Blend my garden, try.

This singing then what for?
   The door, the door, the door:

The emblem of your eye,
   Elizabethan eye.

Landscape

One July morning,
Scumbucket
made an oopsie-woops.

Spilled some paints, I mean.
Ah, the blue!
Oh, the vermilion!

The gold-rompered kid,
ravishing
against the lilies,

sweated it out. Todd
Finkelstein
made a suggestion:

"The new roadsters are
believe you me
the coolest ever."

The angel of the
suburbs sells
indelible stuff.

The oak's that and more.
The spittle-
bug's worth living for,

just the way he foams
all helpless
in his nest of froth

on the pea-green stalk
of the sour
and humble bloodwort.

Among the lesser,
the lessest,
of Earth's filaments,

on the gutter-pipe,
it's Shpidey!
Ragged arachnid

whose chiaroscuro
believe you me
wouldn't start the car.

He

Walked his college girlfriend faithfully to
her masturbation workshop. Factoring in death,
dumped her. The next, a Kisselbaum, read to him from
*Addiction to Perfection: The Still Unravished
Bride.* As a boy, had loved to tell the story
of the low-class Malzbergs hosing off their nude
three-year-old, shit-befouled from chin to ankles,
in full view of the neighborhood kids. Later
won his secondary sex traits and underwent
two separate threesomes. (Many handsome growlings,
but worried: how to give the girls equal fondlings?)
Never could fall asleep with any of them.
Developed a knack but no affection for
physics and non-Euclidean geometry.
The others demanded upscale brunches and
two-armed hugs. He never came right out
and told his uncle (financial analyst) "You've
built a philosophy of your fetishes," but
no way it didn't bother him. Became
attached to dollars, yet cherished a photo of Lake
Ontario in his desk drawer. From time to time,
thought how hassle-free must be the cemetery.
Mortality and sitcoms: his hypnagogics,
those and the slackly leaning winter sunlight.
Embarked on a series of house shares in Fairfield County.
On August nights the oldies mythicized him—
Just two kinds of people in the world.
The roommate-landlord with the mynah bird
foresaw an NPR-soundtracked 90's, declining
to phone a plumber. He fled the mildewed den.
Drove to the public beach at Sherwood Island.
There, throbbing to someone else's boombox, doodling
an explanation of the horizon, conceived
she of the neo-lyric imagination.

Nobody talks about the moon anymore

"Because we have television," my husband says.
"Or because we've been there and know it's only dust."

There's always a full harvest moon on my birthday.
This year I ignored it at the 92nd Street Y

where the presenter, stock-still and mournful, revealed
"without the poetry of Adrienne Rich I would not be

standing here alive today." During the final months
of the trial, Judge Ito insisted that everyone knows the difference

between a waxing and a waning moon, causing lawyers and
spectators to fall into giggles. The moon is not my lady-in-

waiting nor my mother's nacreous teat nor the White Goddess
of life, death, and rebirth, but Sylvia Plath believed it and spent
    far too much

time digging in the craters and coldnesses of her own nervous
    system,
didn't she? Between pathology of intention and loftiness of
    outcome,

I vacillate. Deny her or no, monthly she sends me groaning to
    the Advil bottle.
And I enthuse on my night walks: "Tonight the moon's a gold
    toenail!

My favorite kind!" A massage therapist I met at a party
groused about her friend, whose "reality was a little too
    alternative for me

to deal with." "All our realities are alternative," I pointed out,
"It's only a question of whether they're useful or not,"

but I don't think she "heard" me. A couple of
weeks ago we drove down the West Side Highway

to see a rare performance of *Exiles,* James Joyce's only play,
at St. Mark's Church. There was no moon,

though a hermetic icon incorporating its phases, the numbers 1
through 28, zodiacal symbols and the words *Temptatio* and

Indulgencia was painted on the backdrop. In Act 3
Beatrice and Bertha, who rather ham-fistedly

represent the ethereal Queen of Heaven versus the Earth Mother,
meet in the home of Richard Rowan, the writer

who loves them both, to no one's satisfaction. Bitching,
they approach. Then Bertha draws back her hand

and caresses the face of her rival, clutches her hand.
Breast to breast, declaiming their lines, they

step into their loony, mechanistic waltz across the stage.

The Magic Husband

(1)

Oh, we cavort. *A little less poise, please.*
The shower-crud, the plangent peonies!

He chisels at the oaken escritoire
his paperwork—his toy, his dream, his art—

and hums as if to all America
a dope impromptu on the sound of schwa.

(2)

The shower-crud, the plangent peonies
translate to a grace note, key of E,

which definitely won't be what it should
have been; in fact, will pass away unheard,

but every night at ten my hardy wretch
plays air-piano at the oaken desk.

(3)

With uninvited earnestness he laughs.
He only asked for summer nights sans gnats,

a nap, and freedom from all social roles.
At summer's end he walks the yard and trolls

for squirrel-gnawed pears beneath the fraser fir,
and when he finds them, look, the guy's on fire.

(4)

He came in with the envelope in paw.
He had me read the letter then. I saw

the magic pager on his magic pants,
the wallet full of chits, the triceps tensed,

the pen and pencil set. I had a cry.
Stoop labor, baby. That I'll never try.

(5)

The venture on the Island's fallen through.
Surely the sky shouldn't be that blue.

Has never faded, my true ding an sich,
holdover, throwback, tetchy nihilist

a-muzz with love and narcotherapy.
The tenor wavered contrapuntally,

(6)

the tune bespoke a swan upon a pond.
Even his nerve endings aren't his own.

Sure, I like money. I like lots and lots.
He pitted through his business shirt. He stopped

lightly, lightly, lightly on the steps.
No boy knows just when he goes to sleep.

(7)

The kidskin briefcase trembles at his touch.
We're on a kick with Cherry 7-Up.

How flaky, toxic, wondrous, marginal,
those dulcet suds! He whistles, *Hell was full,*

so I came back. Next afternoon in bed,
he ordered me to spill it so I did.

A Conception

Who wouldn't heave
a careless sigh?
A terror upheld
in sorrow, in rye,

invaded the heart.
The brain took a rest.
The homeopath
proffered his best.

A mystery!
It *did* hurt to try.
It happened then
the usual way:

I got out of bed.
A traffic light blew.
An artery flushed,
a ventricle grew,

lanugo hair
invaded the bog.
The female form
became the norm.

I had to laugh.
The heather went dry.
The grandma cracked
and so did I:

What blare, what bliss
upturns me so?
Who'll cozy to
a mohair throw?

I altered the sauce,
I tasted the bay.
A style was lost
the usual way.

I toddled past
the printed page.
I counted my toes.
I *did* know my age.

The grasses pealed
a tiny reprieve.
I started to read
Emily D.

and waiting for
her stern reply,
the outcome loomed
and so did I.

Nursling

Over there, a fly buzzed—bad.
All ours: the bra, the breast, the breeze.
Starlet of the reciprocal gaze.
Something about her rhymed like mad.

And ours the sigh, the suck, the sing.
We forgave everything we could.
Ravenous palmist. I'm gone for good.
At last I gauged the brash, brash spring.

The skin fiend folded like a fawn.
Torso Magellan. Time's own nub.
Here at the center of the dimmest bulb.
A mouth hovered before latching on.

Babyland

Enter warily: here suavity reigns.
Enter solemnly; enter with great thirst.
Under the banner of the splayed lips, the first baby
staked a claim where the ravine crested and the wax-
white cups of the May flower never shut up.
The second baby failed to live up to its potential,
becoming a charmer who embodied the comic spirit.
At midday, in the dappled thicket,
the third baby simply poured out of you.
The fourth baby, nothing more than a figurehead,
broadcast, in Baltic languages, his many moods.

Step aside: now they come faster and faster.
Newsboy baby delivers the morning paper:
Confessional baby tells all!
Daughter-in-law baby disapproves
and hermit baby is just plain weird.
Sculptor baby lingers over the naughty parts.
A chorus of art critic babies whimpers,
"Why'd they take the tits out of all the pictures?"
Here censorship reigns with its attendant amnesias,
in the desert where the gardenia blooms and in the fen
where vegetable marrows sop up a nutritive fluid.

When night comes the babies scamper into their burrows,
deep under a moonscape of white plains.
Even town crier baby turns in. Nevertheless,
the abandoned square is dominated by a screen
where favorite movies play in an endless loop.
Here reign the sneaky essentials: tread softly
and with respect for the perils you will suffer or cause.
In the blackening copse, for example, a mystery is unfolding—
who, oh who, dropped the final baby?
Little matter, my darlings. Her unrelieved preciousness
would have slain you, just as nature intended.

4

There are that resting, rise.
Can I expound the skies?
How still the Riddle lies!
       —Emily Dickinson

The Search Engine

(after Bishop)

In the city, something beyond me—
I need to know so much.
I scan the boulevards.
I want to find you: where?

To the suburbs come the mailman,
the neighbor lady, the gimp.
They all have one request—
Please, leave your address.

Pebbles plunk in the creek.
Skeeters gasp above.
It seems you've fled the country.
I want to find you: where?

The office park conceals you
in dusty cubicles
and boxes and boxes of files.
Please, leave your address.

The invalids down the shore
find nothing what it was.
The sea will cure most ills
but where to find you, where?

A lean-to by the road,
a quonset near a tree,
a tepee on the sidewalk.
Please, leave your address.

On the movie set, the sidekick
yaps then stops with a jerk.
An extra peeps under the green screen.
I want to find you: where?

Ten thousand average Joes
march on the Capitol.
Dear Representative—
Please, leave your address.

You're a little like a home.
Necessary, too.
I want to find you: where?
Please, leave your address.

Geese on the Median of the Saw Mill Parkway

collect not mottoes but   but notions
   amid the red knobs of
  swamp maple.

Someone gave me the Thunderbird with the mismatched
   hubcaps, someone gives me advice,
    the   the geese give me
  associations—

(O Marianne Moore, you chide, not unfondly, "For
   every time you write a word, you
    feel it twenty, *and* its
  opposite.")

That time in the park by the Hudson, I ruined
   white khakis with the yellow-gray-green
    of their droppings,
  color named

caca d'oie by some   some literalist. A plus:
   their postures, infantine or papal,
    their sloth and donated
  potato chips.

(O Marianne Moore, I honor your finicky
   rigor, but sentiment's all I have!
    "Honks aren't sublime, bird
  or human.")

Safer than V-displays and near escapes to points
   torrid. Let me never forget this
    moment of despair, this
  one, that one,

or t'other. When the blood is up, even virgins
    can fall in love, even   even de-
        pressives resist their stained
    infection

(O Marianne Moore, I am insufficiently
    jazzed by contemporaneity—
        yea, insufficiently
    and then some!)

and Chinese medicine guarantees that because
    nature has gifted us these problems,
        nature will supply the
    solution.

No mottoes, few notions. Marianne, pardon this
    gaggle of worrisome swoops and dips;
        pardon the achings of
    of my taste.

Little America

Pilot truck—follow me. Do you know
what *Tierra Amarrilla* means? She's
called Sophie Dear 'cause she sleeps
on the sofa and runs like a deer. *¡Jesucristo!*

Let's not stay in Gallup. The guide-
book says it's a drinking town. Y'ever been
to the bigass rodeo in Madison Square Garden?
You want that pie hotted up? Good

god, what was that? Just thunder, go
back to sleep. But we didn't discuss this…
I'll take your picture on the yellow line of Route 66.
I'll have the vegetarian Navajo taco.

Taos *sucks*. There's no way I'm climbing
a ladder up that cliff, I'll tell you that right
now. D. H. Lawrence lived in that hut?
I'll be Dave, your masseur. Since we're driving

through Flagstaff, we should try
and find Little America. If I see one
more petrified log, butte, or canyon…
When we were in the Plaza just now, I

saw a really really sad boy at a payphone
with two men too young to be his father.
Gusty winds may exist. I'm not
happy about the underwear situation.

Aquí se puede comprar camisetas perro

(Sign on the gate of Elizabeth Bishop's former house in Key West)

The light was red so we stopped, and
now it is green so we go.
The seabreeze was laparoscopic.

Here's what we worshipped:

A watercolor
whose meaning is clear
but whose import is TBD.

And the casa recalled the perfect progressive!
I had been wishing you a good weekend, a *good* one.

The Flat Tire

The moon was lacquered, more than snide,
and far from round.

The asphalt grew uncivilized
and soon unwound,

the critters filibustering
with clicking sound.

Instead of facile negatives,
her one response:

A briar wood is lovely in
these winter months.

The night was ice and light, and he
assented, once.

>*To act with tangled love could have been*
>*grace indeed.*

>*To handle tangled thoughts? We only*
>*need and need.*

When his regard took on a charge
somehow Ming

she worried how to look at it:
to grasp, or fling—

A joyless interlude or an
ennobled thing?

Into the lull his riposte took
a header then.

Tonight's not what it should have been,
he said again.

A badger braved a truck's highbeams.
He counted ten.

> *To see with tangled words should have been*
> *their new creed.*
>
> *To handle tangled thoughts? We only*
> *need and need.*

A change of heart; and then he thought
he'd change it back.

Beneath the moon the pamphlets in
an awful stack

dwindled nastily and he
misused the jack.

Abstraction paled his pallor, his
goodbye, not good,

flew off in the direction of
the briar wood,

and oil smeared the collar of
his parka hood.

> To act with tangled love could have been
> grace indeed.

> To handle tangled thoughts? We only
> need and need.

The old man's answer—*You can walk.*
It's just a mile—

would complicate his fury with
a not-quite smile

when at his boots the flashlight threw
a crystal tile.

That was something. It was there
a little while.

Three Prayers

Mouth

But we do despise beauty.
We connect it with softness and immortality.
I never sleep at night

but I remember:
a yellow inflatable cat
a waxed church pew

and the long low labor moans.
What's in your—
Get that out of your—
The words have not yet been coined that will fit my—

We woke craving salsa, lemon.
We wandered lonely in the mall.

« »

Chest

Lo, I came in sight of several pelicans
perched on the branches of the mangrove trees.
It was typical weather

for the winter of the year:
a roar at the door
embraceless limbs

cranberries like drops of blood.
To my utmost disappointment,
I saw each pelican, young and old,
leave his perch and take to wing.

I have become timid and hesitant
and live, as it were, mechanically.

And wish to lay me down upon
this superb male whose icon is before me.

« »

Minimus

What will you ask for, other than
a radical openness to persuasion?
Never had we come across

such defiant coziness:
the lush peace of the river
the cuckoo's song

the drifting lazy sky, now blue, now white.
Delicately I crooked my finger.
As delicately, my toe blackened
where I had stubbed it.

New were the uses we found for
our green element.

Ah, that I might have the wings
of a bird. Exactly and only that.

Winter Lyric

Spirit large, life little:
Narrate me down
from here.

Th'organic western wind
a Rothschild land-
lord whose

Olmec sincerity
pontificates
slightly.

Cumuli exceed the
luxe and all it
looks at,

they won't teach history
nor encourage
fancy.

Filigree, be my guide.
Logopoeia,
flense me.

My neurosis, like tea,
cooling in this
weather.

57th Street

(1)

Every second is an automatic door
that you decide to scoot through just in time.

Heading east toward Fifth Avenue,
you pass amethyst earrings, cellular phones,

electronic keyboards, strapped platform shoes,
joss sticks, purple roses, skewered pork

and honeyed cashews, hawkers preaching footrubs,
waiters bearing trays of sorbetto samples,

six lacquered Russian nesting dolls, each disclosing
a littler self, diminishing to a kernel.

The schizzy sputterings of a frazzled bazaar.
You knew something once, a long time ago, yesterday.

(2)

Abased and abashed, your eye works on the world,
a wimpish kind of creation. Isn't there anywhere

to go but forward? You have a millennium
to gestate—no you don't / yes you do. At the greenstand

you savor patchwork of starfruit, pellets of sweet peas,
sliced melons, infant plantains. They brandish price cards;

no one's nude, or tempting you with apples.
A man in fringed suede grabs two fistfuls of peaches,

throws them on the scale. Indifferent,
he'll swing them home, poach them in red wine.

You keep options in a sack over your shoulder.
You have no money, there's nothing you need to buy.

(3)

In front of this sliver building—futuristic,
Coke-bottle-green—a skinny tree fuzzes with buds,

becoming less itself, less the yellow stripling
planted by the Parks Commission. Botany

spends its chemicals, layers of grayness. On the thirty-
third floor, a woman is weeping, moved by her own

bad poems. On fifty, a man tucks the 500 pages
of his science-fiction musical comedy

into a gray cardboard manuscript box.
It's not that you don't love fecundity…

The manuscript box slides into a dresser drawer.
This street—what's the point—how it utters and utters.

(4)

Utterance puffs like dust from the windows of the analyst's
office. Dreams sidle past the Chagall prints, down

the soiled marble stairs. The supplicant
reclines on a vinyl couch, his head resting on

a throwaway cloth. Everything begins here,
in the buzzing brain, and branches nervily out,

and you're either selling it or buying it,
knows the software designer. In a studio, data-bright,

he calculates the end of each choice—
off-on, open-closed, every combination filed—

then encodes them on disks like talismans.
You wish there were one to drop in your pocket.

(5)

Thematic neon palm trees, hot rods, vermin.
Buff pseudo-bouncers. Meta-restaurants vie:

Loll like Rita Hayworth, shake like a Viet-
namese bargirl, sneer like a Shangri-la.

Leather snakes keep odd rosy families on line.
Each father tows a boy with transparent eyes

and promises juice in balloon glasses, snaky french fries.
You will never be a boy, with dyslexia and headlice.

You'll never be that model in a snit
or that lunatic belting *Rule Britannia.*

Children grow up, grownups grow small, what happens
when you get it: a set of Russian nesting dolls.

(6)

You arrive at the corner: trainsets holograms rubies
streamlined jersey dresses. Is this a throng

or is every separate person squinting skyward?
It's a chain reaction. They're excited in Colombian

cottons, in German sandals, in Japanese sunglasses.
Gesticulating, they're anything but laggard.

Do you feel something escape you, like a dream?
The sky, washed in pastel exhausts, conceals

its alien present. What happens when you get it:
you're not a doll, not a program, not a tree?

You're already nostalgic for the twenty-first century.
You tense for the tractable what-happens-next.

Once

In Tokyo, the man sits at a desk, punching a calculator. Nearby his young daughter has taken her sandals off and is biting her toenails. The man's wife has left him to visit her family for a week. Before she left she had been contemptuous; there were money problems between them. He looks up at the wall where his last remaining object of value hangs, a tiny Renoir, very blue. His daughter, missing her mother badly, begins to pluck out her eyelashes and eat them, one by one. She doesn't see, and neither does her father, the stranger behind the door, also peering at the Renoir.

In Lima, the boy walks through a rainstorm. One thought fills him: He doesn't want to be chosen. He has a gang of friends. They're beginning to look at him as a leader. They are sly with hunger. An image of Christ with his apostles besets him. His palms are tingling: will he be stigmatized? The rain lets up, and he is trudging along a beach where he sometimes finds food in the trashcans. He plunges his hands into the sea. A fetus still wearing shreds of blood washes to the shore.

In Hamburg, the techno quartet rehearses the song that will make their names. *Blood and art. Dumb and smart. Love and part.*

In L.A., the girl on the mattress watches a snot-green mandala behind her eyelids. In high school, she'd decided she wanted to be hot. After graduation she took the bus west. A few calls to the wrong people, it wasn't long before she was one of Grady Winn's girls. Grady Winn, super-agent, promises speaking parts but actually hires girls as ambience for his parties. There are four beds, one in each corner of the room, one girl, and one vibrator, on each bed. They come in sequence, as guests eat, drink, and gossip. The girl may be falling in love with Grady Winn. Lately every word she says to him has the hooked quality of a squeal of pleasure. And one of the other girls may be falling in love with her....

Stop this.

In your neighborhood there is a woman. You don't like her because she's more genuine than you. She walks in the evening, sometimes she greets you. You answer without warmth, adding silently *You moron*. Your hateful thoughts follow her up the hill, boring into her back. But one evening, she greets you, and— just this once—you speak to her, kindly.

Riddle

A prism on a tray—
You'll never need a sequel.
The larches lean your way.
A prism on a tray—
Ama-
zing. A stone revel!
A prism on a tray.
You'll never need a sequel.

«»

Plunging into jerkwater,
there's not much to go on.
Fruitless whistlestopper
plunging into jerkwater.
How did this happen, after?
Brain funeral, so on.
Plunging into jerkwater,
there's not much to go on.

«»

You lease, you ply, you chart—
Missing it still is.
The whole pairs not the parts.
You lease, you ply, you chart.
The understanding art
promised more than this.
You lease, you ply, you chart.
Missing it still is.

Rhyme

Then in the caesurae of conversations
  dwarf apple trees perform their grunt work: a patch,
   remembered, in hennaed light. Or, just as well,
    bleach stains on greige carpet, a tabby nicking
     a cheap leather jacket. What tethers them but
      tip-tilt pressure, barometric, slow apart,
       slow together? The answer too plays a part
        in the rhyme if there's a tin ear to hear it.
         Now here comes a tripod massage toy (grinning),
          some raffish diner scents, waxing voluble.
           In this untoward crackle-glass menage, a glitch
            is savvy; perspicacity's violence.

The Nature of Things

(after paintings by Robert Lostutter)

For ages and ages, they couldn't have seemed less simpatico—
street songs turned Brahms's insane cadenza turned sharpening
crack.

Which reminded you of all the novels you might have inhabited,
of your daddy the routeman, of Easter's spice-flavored jelly eggs,
of the rowdy oleander, of the women at the xerox place, so petty.
How privately (you simmered) Time can walk, or fall.

Heart. Couldn't. Break. That was the problem here. A lonely boy.
You were, just.

There must be no self-pity, your pal said then. *And that means NO
self-pity. Can we not do this anymore, please?* Emanation of a wood
fire, blue of blue, singleton, scamp: We live not only in a world
of thoughts, but also in a world of things.

He did you a favor, your pal, when he told you this secret: *First
become ordinary, if you ever wish to become anything else.* By Tuesday,
you were so splendid the bees rose.

The Pleasure of Your Company

Let us go to Tuckahoe.

Let us meet at the duckpond, let us spread a quilt of white eyelet.
Let us throw our shoes at the cygnets. Let us see big things—and
us so small. O breezy decibels. O vin mousseux.

You have a knack for precious communications at crucial
moments. You'll have brought your face towel and your own
nervous mind.

Let us watch the apotheosis, brilliantined, of the seminarian
rounding the pond in his seal-flippered daygown. And the per-
cussionist at her synth-drum, the ice-cream man at his scoop. A
via dolorosa of a radio. The surveyors on their lunch hour, their
badge-like sushi.

Let us steal the act of a genre painting or two. You'll have
become as the moss on the flagstones.

A three-year-old poppet's at work with a lavender sieve. Her au
pair, a pagan in capris. The smell of sunblock, the port-a-potty
spurned....

Let us go to Tuckahoe, please let us go. Let us give pleasure, let
us relieve guilt, let us facilitate perception. This most important:
Let us have not gravity but its illusion.

The clouds have a fire within them. The underbrush stirs. Let us
shelter in a damp Camaro. Let the poppet surrender her doll to
the waters.

Now a dove dives and now you revile the way you're not tasty
unless kissed, not gorgeous until beheld. O easy lyricism, O cask
of Poupon. Now to rededicate this Delft world we live in.

NOTES

"Ballade Confessionnelle" is composed of lines from the poetry of Sylvia Plath and Anne Sexton.

The title "Nobody talks about the moon anymore" is a line from "String of Pearls," a poem by Randall D. Marshall.

Sources for "Three Prayers": the novels of John Galsworthy; *The Art of Fiction* by John Gardner; *Proverbs; Birds of America* by John James Audubon; poems by Sylvia Plath and Elizabeth Bishop; Vincent Van Gogh's letters.

Title and some phrases from "The Nature of Things" are taken from a catalogue of Robert Lostutter's paintings.

In "The Pleasure of Your Company" the words "give pleasure…relieve guilt… facilitate perception" come from Simon Lesser's essay on the functions of form in art. Ezra Pound's *Cantos* are the source for "The clouds have a fire within them. The underbrush stirs."

KATHLEEN OSSIP was born in Albany, New York. Her poems have appeared in *The Best American Poetry 2001*, as well as in many journals, including *The Paris Review* and *The Kenyon Review*. She teaches at the New School University in New York City.